Not Heavy, Just Awkward

NOT HEAVY
just awkward

SCOTT GIBSON

WITH CONTRIBUTIONS FROM LINDSAY GIBSON GOINS

Original Lyrics by Scott Gibson

Cover Images Courtesy of Jennifer Leonard and Christopher Allred

Back Cover Description by Donnie Roberts

ISBN: 978-1-387-85039-6

Whatever may come of any of this, know that you are the inspiration.

SG
January 2, 2015

CONTENTS

Foreword 9

Introduction 13

A Postcard: Lexitown and Other Observations
Lexitown 16
The Watcher 20
Go Tell Mama 22
City Council Man 25
Old Dirt Road..29
I Wanna Be An Apeman 31
Steel in Love..34
Talkin' Changes...37
The Firemen of Engine No. 2...39
Down on the Line...43
Waitin' for the Bomb to Fall..47
The Ballad of Maggie Taylor..50
Down at the Candy Factory..53
The Load...57

Intermission: "The Poetry Corner"
Vowel Movement..60

The Essential Scott Gibson
Won't Be Tread Upon..64
Breakin' My Mind All the Time.......................................66
Blue Jay 68
Hey, Driver 70
Desire is a Flame...73
Like a River...75
Babylon Jail...78

Sad to Cry 81
Ball and Chain 83
Hey Johnny, Git Yer Gun..86
Jihad Blues..88
Time, Time, Time 90
There Once Was a Man..94
Hail, Oceania 97
Table of the Lord 100

"Scott-isms", Wisdom, and Woe
A Note On "Scott-isms" 104

Afterword 133

Acknowledgements 137

FOREWORD
by Lindsay Gibson Goins

I had no idea that my dad had written a book until a few days after his passing. Our friend, Chris Phelps, told me that my dad had given him the only printed copy several years ago. Chris told me that when he attempted to return the book, my dad said he should keep it so perhaps he could "get it into the right hands one day". I don't believe it was mine that he was talking about, but rather the hands of his listeners. I'm simply the middle-man; my purpose is to facilitate the handoff.

See, my dad wrote for all of you. You conservatives, you liberals, you poor folk, you rich folk, you mothers, you fathers, you children, you believers, you non-believers, you politicians, you small business owners, you family members, you friends, you strangers, you loners, you socialites, you wayward souls, you kindred spirits, you... people. Every one of *you*.

If my dad's music had to be placed into a category, it would simply be the genre of life, set to lyrics and chords, written to reflect and mimic the lives of those who listen.

When I thought about publishing my dad's book, I decided I wanted to change as little as possible. I want you to feel like you're reading the original version, frozen in time. I've edited the text slightly to ensure the Grammar Police won't be making any arrests (hopefully), and I've formatted the printed lyrics a bit to coincide with the audio. The order of the songs has been rearranged so you'll be able to follow along as you listen. My vision for this book is not perfection, but rather a perfect example of imperfection.

My dad didn't talk about the meaning or inspiration behind his lyrics very much. I think this is because he felt he was just the messenger; he wanted people to gather their own interpretations. However, this book shines a light on his personal thoughts associated with each song. From the motivation behind *There Once Was a Man*, to the history of *The Ballad of Maggie Taylor*, and even a glimpse at the recording of *Time, Time, Time...* this book will certainly help you bridge the gap between my dad's lyrics and the messages within them. Think of it as a "cheat code" for listening to Scott Gibson's music.

Although he never said it, I feel like my dad would've wanted his book and first two albums (*A Postcard: Lexitown and Other Observations* and *The Essential Scott Gibson*) to be experienced simultaneously. Of course, there is no wrong way to read this book, but the cynical jokester in my dad would probably have suggested that you listen to a song, ponder its meaning, then read his explanation so you can see just how different your perception is from his own.

At the conclusion of this book, you'll find a compilation of journal entries, lyrics, quotes, poetry, and prose in a section I've entitled, *"Scott-isms", Wisdom, and Woe*. I doubt the content is anything my dad would be particularly proud of, but I treasure it just the same. I think you will, too.

The name of this book is one that my dad was playing around with for one of his albums. His original manuscript was untitled, but I decided <u>Not Heavy, Just Awkward</u> was an appropriate title to adorn the final product; I believe it has just the right combination of obscurity and undeniable certainty.

Literally speaking, *heavy* means something is difficult to move because of its weight. Likewise, *awkward* means something is difficult to move because of its design. You can take the bricks out of a box to make it lighter, but you can't change the shape or size of the box itself. You must find an alternate strategy – work a little harder and think a little smarter – if you intend for the box to move. It may be uncomfortable, but it'll be worth it in the end.

Figuratively speaking, I believe this is a term to describe the feeling you get when something is really tough, in the sense that you simply weren't designed to obtain or understand it. It's not an excuse, but a challenge, or call to action.

Friend and loyal fan, Bruce Wehrle, wrote, "[Scott's] philosophies on life were gentle, observant, and rational, even if they came at you from perhaps a slightly shifted angle. He could make you think about something profound even before you knew you were thinking about it. That was the artist in him."

Friend and fellow musician, William VonReichbauer, added, "He was utterly fearless, musically... He was like a carpenter with a box full of tools, choosing just the right one to best carve a piece from sound rather than wood."

Bandmate and friend, Scott Eppinga, observed, "He had the ability to make you forget your troubles and laugh, or make you think of what was really important."

Due to the overall consensus, many would claim that Scott Gibson himself was "not heavy, just awkward". I believe the greatest impact of his work is yet to be made. Or maybe not. But one thing is certain... you are reading his book right now. And that, my friend, is enough to make a difference.

I'd like to thank my dad for his contribution to the world, to our community, to us "folk"... to me. I hope you'll "hear" his voice throughout this book, and perhaps feel a connection to him through his words. Join me in keeping his legacy alive by carrying his music in your heart... today, and always.

INTRODUCTION

Why a book? I can't imagine. But maybe we will both discover the answer before this introduction is finished.

Songwriting comes naturally to me; writing books does not. One would think the two very similar since they both involve transposing thoughts into words and sentences. But for me, at least, there is a huge difference. A song has a media or pattern on which the words can be placed, and although that media is an art form in itself and can be changed or tweaked as needed, there is still a sense of order that's always present. Freestyle writing, or whatever this type of effort is called, has less of a pattern, or order, and has to be approached differently.

An artist can use paint and canvas to create a work of art. He can also use clay to sculpt another. The canvas, while totally open to any type of emotion or ideas the artist might smear upon it, has dimension, shape, size, a top, sides, and a bottom. But a mound of clay on a table is a different media altogether. It's just as respondent to the artist's every whim, but no real pattern or dimension holds it in place other than the gravity of Earth, which holds us all in its grasp.

I enjoy this type of writing, but am less comfortable doing it than I am with song. I am less comfortable because I am more vulnerable, and I instinctively sense it. In songwriting, I very quickly know where I want to go with the end product. The idea forms in more of a "big picture", leaving me to merely decode and translate it into a musical message.

This type of writing is similar. It's more like dictation, except that I'm trying to keep pace with my own thoughts. There is less time to think or weigh the consequences, like those embarrassing moments we all have when something comes out of our mouths suddenly. It does so without first passing through the brain... a straight shot from the well of emotions. See... there it is! And not only was I powerless to stop it, I never even saw it coming. Cool and extremely interesting, but at the same time, so very revealing and invading.

It is my hope that this book will not only answer a few questions, but replace them with new ones. I hope it evokes thought but will not stifle or discourage it. I hope you are entertained, that you laugh, and maybe cry, if it serves a good purpose.

Thank you for the gift of your time. Believe me, I fully realize just how valuable and precious that gift is.

A Postcard: Lexitown and Other Observations

LEXITOWN

"And what kind of music do you play, man?"

"Folk music."

"Folk music, you say? What does it sound like?"

"Well, it tells a story… kinda like rap or country. It sounds a little like bluegrass, except slower. And you don't really have to be any kind of musician or singer to do it… kinda like pop."

"Oh, can you play *Freebird*?"

"Well, uh, no, but if you'll give me three minutes, I'll try and explain what folk music is. Folk music is music about people and the circumstances and events that affect us."

"Have you started yet? Because if all you're going to do is talk, I know what that sounds like."

"Let me play this for ya… *Lexitown, Lexitown, jobs all gone in Lexitown…*"

"Oh, well, why didn't you just say that you write socially conscious material, set to music based on traditional arrangements, and perform your songs using mainly instruments familiar to that classic era?"

"Is that what I do?"

"Sounds like it to me."

"Thanks."

16

"Anytime. You sure you don't know *Freebird*?"

"What does it sound like?"

Lexitown

Lexitown, Lexitown
Little bit of heaven is Lexitown
Prettiest place you ever found
I love Lexitown

Lexitown, Lexitown
Born and raised in Lexitown
Golden rule won't let you down
God bless Lexitown

Lexitown, Lexitown
Met a little gal in Lexitown
Gonna get married and settle down
Down in Lexitown

Hey, Lexitown, Lexitown
Easy pickin's in Lexitown
Plenty of jobs all around
Good luck, Lexitown!

Lexitown, Lexitown
Keep your eye on Lexitown
Nose in the air, ear to the ground
What's up, Lexitown?

Lexitown, Lexitown
Jobs all gone in Lexitown
Boss says, "Son, gotta shut 'em down!"
Too bad, Lexitown

Well, Lexitown, Lexitown
Busted flat in Lexitown
Gimmie five dollars, I'm Heaven bound
So long, Lexitown

THE WATCHER

It is the solemn task of every generation to be the keepers of the past, mingle it with the present, and then pass it on to the future.

If this is done with meticulous care and reverence to the truth, the result can only be a positive force for the betterment of humanity.

If it's done with no regard to truth and changed to suit the agendas of each generation, the result will only hinder any progress, but eventually produce a creature who has no idea who they are, where they have come from, or where it is they should go.

Those seeking to alter the truth for their own gain are the worst kind of thieves and scoundrels. They soil the past, manipulate the present, and give their own children a legacy that dooms them to repeat the same mistakes over and over and over again.

The Watcher

Well, he stands straight and tall on the platform
Stands there in sun, and wind, and rain
And he keeps a watcher's eye
From his post up in the sky
And never does he sigh or complain

Some say that he come from Carolina
Others say he come from Tennessee
From Georgie, Alabam'
Savannie, Birmin'ham
Truth is, he came from you and me

He's a military man without question
His musket rifle firm in his hand
And he never questioned why
When they sent him out to die
In defense of his family and his land

Yes, he fought for the cause as he knew it
And he fought for his chill'un and his wife
Neither cursed, nor condoned
What is right, what is wrong
But only to preserve his way of life

He was silent as the years rolled slowly by him
And he's seen the generations come and go
He's just waiting for the day when all hate will fade away
From the people who pass him from below

So, he stands as a symbol to all people
A tribute to those who fought and died
Will you honor him today, or just turn your head away?
He leaves it up to you to decide

GO TELL MAMA

Through many wars and many battles, sons of mothers have fought, bled, and died on fields of honor.

This song is dedicated to them.

It has no agenda, offers no opinion, and asks no questions.

It is only a moment of ear-piercing silence dedicated to those who have fallen... or will fall.

Go Tell Mama

Go tell Mama her blue-eyed son's
A-comin' home from the war
But please don't tell her I don't look
The way I did before

Tell her I was brave and strong
On the battlefield that day
When a white-hot piece of a cannon ball
Took my blue eyes away

Go tell Mama her red-haired son's
A-comin' home from the war
But please don't tell her that I don't look
The way I did before

Just tell her that my heart was pure
In the jungle on that day
When the orange dust of a chemical cloud
Took my red hair away

Go tell Mama her ramblin' boy's
A-comin' home from the war
Please don't tell her that I can't ramble
The way I did before

Just tell her that my path was true
In the desert on that day
I was first in line when they tripped the mine
That took my two legs away

Go tell Mama her only son's
A-comin' home from the war
Please don't tell her I won't be back
The way I was before

Just tell her that I love her
And I'll see her bye 'n' bye
And that for some to live in freedom
Others have to die

CITY COUNCIL MAN

One of the things that really intrigues me about folk music is the totally unselfish approach that its "salesmen" exhibit toward one another. If there is any competition between fellow singers/writers, it's viewed as a "family thing" and never expressed as arrogant or hurtful.

While other forms of art usually view a direct copy of a work or term as piracy, folk artists seem to embrace the notion and actually encourage it.

Many examples of one simple tune being used by various artists as a vehicle for their original lyrics are there to see. It's like somebody starts off a song, then passes it over to the next fellow who in turn adds his own bit, then passes it to the next guy in line.

My feeling is the whole concept of folk is like a brotherhood of sorts, with a higher, larger collective goal that all involved share in advancing and promoting.

City Council Man took me down this highway like a pilgrim standing on the side of the road, flagging a ride from a dustbowl Okie on his way to the promised land. The story is straight out of the local news, and I could have told it in many ways, but as the idea began to form, I thought it only fitting to seek the help of the Master of the Social Protest Song... Woody Guthrie.

His anthem of abuse, *Vigilante Man*, has always been a favorite of mine because of the light-hearted, almost comical way he chose to tell his tale of violence and woe. There is usually some bit of humor to be found in the way people aggravate each other, and the best way to set about mending things might just be to pull that humor out and shake it around a bit.

They say that one of the most influential and necessary people to be found at a king's court of old was the jester. A certified fool whose "lot" was to inject a bit of humor into situations that were getting a bit too heated to produce positive results. Well, everybody's gotta be something, I guess.

Thanks, Woody. God bless. Let's do it again sometime.

City Council Man

Have you seen that City Council Man?
Have you seen that City Council Man?
Have you seen that City Council Man?
Been hearin' his name cussed all over the land

Well now, what is a City Council Man?
Tell me, what is a City Council Man?
Does he rob you blind, does he annex up your land?
Yeah, that's a City Council Man

Yesterday as I stood out on my step
Saw a man in little white hat
He's drawin' crooked lines on a map
Was that a City Council Man?

Tell me, what is a City Council Man?
Tell me, what is a City Council Man?
Does he rob you blind, does he annex up your land?
Yeah, that's a City Council Man

Once I had me a shop this side of town
Put me up a sign to bring my business 'round
Man came by, he made me tear it down
Was that a City Council Man?

When I die and they lay me in the ground
Put two coins on my eyes to keep my eyelids down
Please double-check 'fore you lower me down
In case the City Council come 'round

Tell me, what is a City Council Man?
Tell me, what is a City Council Man?
Does he rob you blind, does he annex up your land?
Yeah, that's a City Council Man

OLD DIRT ROAD

There are two kinds of people in the word. There are those who lived on dirt roads when they were children… and those who didn't.

There's an automatic kinship between folks who have ever lived on one and the sights, sounds, feels, and smells are all the subject of endless conversation when they meet. The reference in this song to "hoppy toads" and "summer rains" with mud squishing up between your toes are as strong as blood when it comes to binding folks together and finding community. I usually ask the audience, who among them are "dirt roadies", and make it a point to watch for their reaction to the references. I have seen tears, smiles, and more than one inhale at the very mention of "honeysuckle".

The last verse tells of a different time. A time when dirt roads become paved and simplistic, childhood wonders become complicated, adult problems. But us Road Folk do have an advantage over others when life deals us those "heavy blows" and things get too complex to understand or cope with.

All it takes is a smell, or a feel, or the faint echo of an imaginary supper call to instantly lift us from the hot, sticky problems of life and land us entry into a softer, cooler place, somewhere on the dirt road in our minds.

Old Dirt Road

Took off a-walkin' down that old dirt road
Barefoot, jumpin' like a hoppy toad
I can feel the mud in between my toes
Time is movin' slow
Down on that old dirt road

Early in the mornin', old dirt road
Blackberry pickin' with a paper poke
Mama makin' pie with brown sugar dough
Time is movin' slow
Down on that old dirt road

The honeysuckle, the summer rain
A supper-time call, a child's refrain
The mourning dove, the whip-poor-will
Know exactly how you feel

Late in the evenin', old dirt road
Yonder comes a mama with the young'uns in tow
Tryin'a make it home for the sun gets low
Life is moving slow
Down on that old dirt road

Every now and then when I'm feelin' low
Life is dealin' me a heavy blow
A voice calls out from within my soul
And beckons me to go
Back to that old dirt road

I WANNA BE AN APEMAN

It's all about heroes and simple, uncomplicated living. No shoes, no haircuts, no problems.

This one is a crowd pleaser no matter what type of audience I serve it to. The lyrics – a total brain-spasm and electric daydream that will have the toughest construction worker beating his chest and shouting out whatever apeman "yell" rang out from the screen at the Saturday matinee when he was a kid.

There is a lot we can learn from the scene in the first Weissmuller movie where he and Jane Parker are attempting to communicate.

"Tarzan... Jane, Jane ...Tarzan."
"Tarzan... Jane, Jane... Tarzan... Ungawa!"

In a perfect world, no sentence would need to contain any more than three words followed by, "Ungawa!"

I Wanna Be an Apeman

Well, I'm just about to get sick and tired
Of livin' in the human race
Everybody pushin', shovin' me around
And gettin' down in my case
So I'm gettin' out while the gettin's good
My mama didn't raise no fool
If you can slow down to the speed of sound
I'll tell you what I'm gonna do

I wanna be an apeman, livin' in the trees
Nothin' to do but swing around the jungle
With a monkey hangin' on my knees
I wanna be an apeman, listen what you oughta do
If you could only get yourself together
You could be an apeman, too

Well I've spent the whole first half of my life
Tryin' to get ahead
Wake up every morning, read the 'bituary column
To see if I'm alive or dead
The thing that's gettin' me down the most
About copin' with society
Is knowin' in the world's a couple billion people
Tryin' to cope with me, so…

I wanna be an apeman, livin' in the trees
Nothin' to do but swing around the jungle
With a monkey hangin' on my knees
I wanna be an apeman, listen what you oughta do
If you could only get your stuff together
You could be an apeman, too

I wanna be an apeman, livin' in the trees
Nothin' to do but swing around the jungle
With a monkey hangin' on my knees
I wanna be an apeman, listen what you oughta do
If you could only get yourself together
You could be an apeman, too

STEEL IN LOVE

Such and amazing and unique word... *love*.

On its own, the word is like a pure, blank canvas. It's the perfect receptor for expression, but without a clear expression of its own.

You can indeed love espresso coffee and, at the same time, love your family. However, it is the object of that affection – the picture painted on that blank canvas – that brings the word to life and gives it power and intensity.

The classification process is only the first step. The next test is one that separates the pure and true from the impure and false. It is the process, that in all of nature, is the most effective means of rendering something to its purest form – the application of heat, pressure, or friction. It seems anything considered valuable or strong has either been heated, pressed, or abraded by natural or man-made means in order to become that way.

Concrete, glass, and copper can indeed make for a beautiful building. But unless that building has an internal structure of hardened steel, the building will topple when the winds of adversity howl and the Earth shakes around it. Sometimes it's obvious to the beholder, but more times than not, the steel is hidden away on the inside, vigilantly performing its necessary task.

It seldom gets any recognition; no beautiful adornments or inspirational words. That honor is usually left for the more superficial materials, the ones that sparkle and shine and appear fast and immovable.

That steel wasn't just picked up off the ground or gouged out of a hole and bolted together to form the foundation. First, it had to be heated by an intense fire so the impurities that may potentially weaken it could be burned away. Then, it was poured out to cool and hammered into a sturdy, beam-worthy material.

Love is like that as well.

Steel in Love is my way of saying that love has been tempered by the fire and tested by the storm.

Steel in Love

She's a three-time loser, workin' on number four
He lives in a house made of cards, without any door
I feel sorry for him, his love's never been tried
Don't know what it's like to go through a storm
And come out on the other side

      Steel in love, steel in love
      Steel in love, steel in love

She keeps a candle burnin' in the window of her mind
She keeps her sexu'l frustrations all bottled up inside
When I come home this Friday
It'll all be better, like I said it would be
I'll kiss you once, and I'll kiss you again
Together through eternity

      Steel in love, steel in love
      Steel in love, steel in love

He's ridin' in the fast lane, he's a hundr'd miles from home
His mind wanders back to a year ago
And it chills him to the bone
But he knows she's waitin'
And he knows who she's waitin' for
And she'll want him back, in spite of the fact
He lost his legs in the war

      Steel in love, steel in love
      Steel in love, steel in love

TALKIN' CHANGES

Talkin' changes is a result of makin' choices. We all make 'em every day. Matter of fact, who we are is nothing but the sum of every single choice we've ever made.

The mindblower is that the very next choice you make could change everything.

Choose wisely, my friend.

Talkin' Changes

Out of the black and into the white
Into the day, out of the night
Out of the wrong, into the right
Tomorrow is just another word for never

Out of the back door, into the front
Don't be afraid, come on, jump!
Stairs going down, stairs going up
And "maybe" is just another word for "no"

Out of the back door and into the street
Blow a holy kiss to everyone I meet
But they all turn and look at me like I'm crazy

Up from the fake, into the real
Out of the numb, into the feel
Chop some wood, cook some steel
And sacrifice is just another word for love

In from the cold and into the heat
Into a home out of the street
Throw down the crutch, stand on your feet
And pride is just another word for longing

Out of the old, into the new
Leave the many and join the few
Forget the lies, seek the truth
And being born is just another word for dying

THE FIREMEN OF ENGINE NO. 2

I was uptown one day, I believe on a Friday, though I can't actually recall, and came to light on the steps of the old courthouse. That in itself isn't very odd; I do that often and have since I was a teen growing up in "Lexitown". But on that particular day I was unusually interested and had an overwhelming urge to check out the museum. I had just finished penning *The Watcher* and felt I could pick up some "icing" there or maybe The Dude himself was sending out a vibe... who knows.

I went inside and was immediately bombarded by the sensation that I had been taken back through time to another era. My mind raced and evoked images of strangely-dressed people going about their day-to-day business that would bring them into the county seat courthouse.

A nice lady soon appeared and I was whisked away to the exhibit hall and given a rather cool and knowledgeable tour of the artifacts on display. One of the first items to catch my eye was a crimson-colored fire alarm box attached to a wooden pole. There was nothing strange about the alarm box, as there were many of them in service when I was a kid ripping up and down Main Street, but it was odd to see it there, suspended in the air on a sawed-off bit of old phone pole.

The magic started as the lady began to tell the tale of how one of Lexington's two fire trucks was involved in a wreck back in 1926 and how three firefighters met their doom on that fateful day. The added fact that the tragedy was set into motion by a false alarm, given on that very alarm box, just put me into orbit. Brother, this was like throwing a hambone to a hound dog. I was on it and had the lyrics in less than a day.

As I started the task of scoring the music, thoughts of the heritage and history of firefighting haunted me and the vision of early Irish immigrants, down from the mountains for the mill jobs, rang out like a bell. The main body of the music drones like a melancholy pipe and just when the story line gets heavy and needs a bit of that famous Irish levity, the chorus chimes into a major-chord pub sing-a-long.

I'm proud of this tune, not as a reflection of me, but because it has the potential to live on for years and years, doing its job, telling the tale of the brave ones who put their lives on the line for us. The last verse... well, I just couldn't resist the urge to add a bit of mystery.

The Firemen of Engine No. 2

On the first of January, 1926
The call come to the firehouse, help was needed quick
The good boys fired their engine for the second time that day
As they rolled out of the station, you could hear the people say

Here's to the firemen of Engine Number Two
The good boys, the strong boys, the brave, and the true
Now and forever, we sing to honor you
The firemen of Engine Number Two

As they headed up the main street, toward the center square
Their siren was a-blarin' to warn the people there
At a New Year's celebration at the theater uptown
The party had just ended, yeah, and the crowd was all around

Well, there is no blame to lay here, what happened on that night
The car came from the left side, they were lookin' right
First, the sound of rubber, and then the sound of steel
Then the sound of prayin' as the driver cut his wheel

Here's to the firemen of Engine Number Two
The good boys, the strong boys, the brave, and the true
Now and forever, we sing to honor you
The firemen of Engine Number Two

There were two that could've died there, but walked away instead
And two that lay there injured, three that lay there dead
Daniel Cope and Eddie and Howard Michael, gone
But Henry Yarborough and "Freight Train" Gibson
Lived to carry on

Now, the next day they discovered, at alarm box twenty-six
The call that came that faithful night, nothin' but a trick
A false alarm was sounded by a shadow in the dark
There never was a fire that night, never was a spark

Now, the old folks say that shadow still walks the streets at night
Lookin' to do penance, and a'tryin' to make it right
And they say that if you listen on the first night of each year
The sound of a single ghostly siren you might hear

Here's to the firemen of Engine Number Two
The good boys, the strong boys, the brave, and the true
Now and forever we sing to honor you
The firemen of Engine Number Two

Here's to the firemen of Engine Number Two
The good boys, the strong boys, the brave, and the true
Now and forever, we sing to honor you
The firemen of Engine Number Two

DOWN ON THE LINE

If someone could invent a pair of glasses – a viewer, of sorts – that could "see" all the many lines we humans draw to distinguish right from wrong, good from bad, proper from improper, normal from abnormal, the image would surely be one of more lines than space in between the lines, and overwhelm the senses of anyone trying to see through them.

We all draw them. It's perfectly natural to do so, and in most cases, is a positive gesture, since it helps keep us on "this side" of situations and behaviors that we instinctively sense as harmful or improper. Society and culture also draw their own set of lines based on some sort of collective idea of what is negative or unacceptable. Religion is another architect the adds its own lines to the mix. So, in essence, our concept of what we do, say, and even think, is governed by whether or not our actions cross any of those lines.

Some people seem to have no problem keeping a fair distance away from any line, while others seem to constantly be crossing them. So much, in fact, that they basically live beyond the lines set down by society as acceptable.

But most of us fall into a third category – people who know what's right, or proper, but still find themselves straddling those lines on occasion. That, too, is natural – and human – and usually results in a correction that sets us back at a proper distance.

Probably the most pitiful of folks are those who, no matter how hard they might try, always seem to find themselves weaving and bobbing back and forth directly on those lines. They essentially "live" in a place that, for most people, is the ultimate place of inner torment and conflict. Even those who choose to dwell on the other side of the line seem to have more peace than the ones who lie directly on it.

I know people like that; I'm sure you do as well, and sometimes they aren't easy to approach, or help. We naturally hesitate because we know that to help them, we must first go to where they live... down on The Line. And to go there is to put ourselves in a position where our own strength may be tested.

Down on the Line

Listen to the sound of that freight train
Rollin' down the Tennessee line
I swear, that whistle is a-callin' my name
And it beckons me back one more time

Some people live in a mansion
With crystal and linens so fine
Some people live by the sweat of their brow
But a Lineman lives on The Line

Listen, and I'll tell my story
Listen while I still have my mind
My story is true, and I'll tell it to you
To keep you from a life on The Line

I left from the town of my childhood
My mama and daddy, so kind
I took all the money they had saved all their life
And squandered it down on The Line

Some people live in a mansion
With crystal and linens so fine
Some people live by the sweat of their brow
But a Lineman lives on The Line

I met a young girl from the country
Who came here with stars in her eyes
She gave up her virtue, her hopes, and her dreams
For the bright lights down on The Line

Then I met an old man at the station
He was dirty and stinkin' of wine
I looked in his looking-glass eyes, and I saw
My future, down on The Line

Now, some people live in a mansion
With crystal and linens so fine
And some people live by the sweat of their brow
But a Lineman lives on The Line

Yes, a Lineman lives on The Line

WAITIN' FOR THE BOMB TO FALL

I can remember an evening as a child when some relatives and neighbors came by to visit. Now, this in itself wasn't unusual at all, but the looks on their faces and the way they kinda whispered and hushed each other was. It scared me. I don't know why, but I guess it was because I sensed fear in them, and that was something I wasn't used to.

I remember hearing the words "president" and "bombs" and "Russians", but not much more. Didn't need to hear more. The concern on the faces of people I knew to be completely fearless was enough to send me packing to the sack when Mama said, "Go!"

The next day, things seemed better, and in a week or so, pretty much back to normal… but never really the same.

Of course, the event that shook everybody up so much was the showdown of nuclear powers known today as the Cuban Missile Crisis of 1962.

I had pretty much missed the Cold War, but it didn't have much presence in Davidson County, anyway. However, I did hear later about the people who built bomb shelters in their back yards and how it was common to have drills in schools where the students were instructed on how to best prepare for an attack.

Today, we live under similar strains. The threat of violence is indeed real and deadly. But there was a difference back then. Today's violent acts, or attacks, are more contained, more isolated; even through the destruction of life is just as sure, the potential to dodge the bullet is there as well.

In the 1960's, an "attack" pretty much meant a nuclear attack, and one that very few, if any, would be spared from. Looking back, I can truly see that period as the pivotal point that was to propel us later into the "Live for Today, Damn Tomorrow" culture that we've become. It's human nature, I guess.

It's troubling as I watch the news and see the number of nations obtaining nuclear "power". I just hope we realize that the 60's were a different time when nations had different agendas and temperaments … and fears.

I hope we have the good sense not to expect the same outcome of the standoffs of that time. I hope we have the good sense to be afraid.

Waitin' for the Bomb to Fall

Hammer is on the sickle
Graffiti on the wall
Everybody sittin' with their heads in their knees
Waitin' for the bomb to fall

Clown is on the TV
Havin' himself a ball
Rich man prayin' to his rosary
Waitin' for the bomb to fall
And we don't see the madness of it all

Elvis has left the building
Nikita's on the stall
Kennedy rockin' in his rockin' chair
Waitin' for the bomb to fall

Bird Lady's face is cold and pale
Lookin' like a China doll
Cowboy lettin' his hair grow long
Waitin' for the bomb to fall
And we don't see the madness of it all

Rich man sittin' in his hole in the ground
He don't care at all
Thinkin' 'bout his place in the world to come
Waitin' for the bomb to fall

Devil is sittin' on a mountain top
Havin' himself a ball
God just standin' there shakin' his head
Waitin' for the bomb to fall
And we don't see the madness of it all

THE BALLAD OF MAGGIE TAYLOR

The ladies seem to really identify with this one. I guess the hardship of past generations still chime a chord in women, even today. There are indeed common factors that act as the tie that binds folks – even over time and innovation, or progress. That's a good thing, I suppose.

My ancestors were working folk, still are. Down from the mountains to the farms, and then to the factories and mills of the Piedmont; it was a hard life that didn't offer much in the way of an escape. However, they did alright for poor folk.

Back then, being poor didn't mean you qualified for government assistance... it meant you were poor. It meant that you had to do without many of the things that are considered necessities of life today. Somehow, life went on... but sometimes it didn't.

It's hard to get across to some of the younger folk that there was a time when children walked straight from elementary school into the cotton mill to put in another few hours of work before supper. Or a father who worked all week, but after he passed through the company store, paid his weekly bills, and purchased a few groceries, he may only have had thirty cents left from his pay.

It's an important story to tell, and I will tell it as long as I am able, for those who lived selfless lives for their children, and their children's children, to have better ones.

Those are lives that need to be remembered and celebrated and respected. Maggie Taylor is one of those lives. Her story is true, her hardship real, her legacy proud, and her children's children better because of her.

Margaret Taylor Gibson Hunt… rest now for a spell.

Note: For those unfamiliar with the term, "Arsh taters" are simply boiled potatoes with thickening in the broth to make them go a bit farther on the table. "Arsh" is country for Irish. A "widder's weed" is country slang for a widow's weed, or suit of clothes worn during a time of mourning. Usually it was worn by a wife mourning her husband's death.

The Ballad of Maggie Taylor

Married in the summer of nineteen-hundred-five
Workin' in the cotton mills, two shifts at a time
Eatin' Arsh taters just to try to stay alive
He's a-gone, Maggie Taylor, he's a-gone

Yeah, he's a-gone, Maggie Taylor, he's a-gone

She was only fourteen when the babies came along
First one, then another, 'till her bearin' days was gone
But somethin' died inside her when the twins was taken home
He's a-gone, Maggie Taylor, he's a-gone

Yeah, he's a-gone, Maggie Taylor, he's a-gone

The cotton crop is dyin', the mills a-gettin' lean
Ain't no time for cryin', you got hungry mouths to feed
And gal, it won't be long 'till you wear that widder's weed
He's a-gone, Maggie Taylor, he's a-gone

Yeah, he's a-gone, Maggie Taylor, he's a-gone

It was in November when Paw took to his bed
"He'll soon get better," that's what the doctor said
But then he got the fever, in three days he was dead
He's a-gone, Maggie Taylor, he's a-gone

Yeah, he's a-gone, Maggie Taylor, he's a-gone

DOWN AT THE CANDY FACTORY

I guess I was a pretty good kid, not prone to too much mischief. Well, no more than any other red-blooded, American boy. But on the occasion that I did have a slight misjudgment in behavior that resulted in the standard punishment handed out by the loving, but stern, teachers at Holt Elementary School, I usually took advantage of the few minutes between being released from after-school detention and being picked up by my mom by sneaking next door to the Piedmont Candy Company.

I don't recall ever being treated like I was imposing, although I'm sure I was. Even kids can pick up on that, but I never felt it. All I remember were nice people dressed in white with paper "army" hats, going about the task of making candy. It was, at least in my eyes, a scene straight out of *Willy Wonka*. Workers were scurrying about, mixing and cooking their sugary goo, rolling and feeding it into a machine that magically transformed it into a long rope of red-stripped goodness, ready to be cut into sticks and packaged into that famous box with the red birds on it. The payoff was a small, brown paper bag of broken pieces that was handed to me as I left to see mom and face the music for whatever I had done to merit staying after school.

As I said, I wasn't a bad kid, so the "music" usually wasn't too bad, either. Likewise, the added bribe of a piece of my candy didn't hurt my situation. As things would have it, my mom was also a fan of the peppermint sticks and had enjoyed them when she was a kid. Sometimes it's the simplest of things that seem to transcend over time and space and bring generations of people together.

As I perform this song and the names of all the candy in my "bag" spill out, I never fail to see a smile when someone else's favorite is mentioned. My favorite? I do have a passion for candy corn, but the one that affects my soul about as much as it does my sweet tooth is a stick of Red Bird peppermint.

An extra-special treat that has been passed down through at least four generations in my own family is to take a stick of Red Bird Peppermint and poke it into an orange that was first rolled a bit to release the juice. The flavor of the tangy orange juice being sucked through the cool peppermint candy is truly the most unique and wondrous taste known to man.

Down at the Candy Factory

Well, when I was a young'un and a-runnin' around
I'd save my pennies for the trip to town
Mama'd be runnin' errands all around
And I'd get tired and begin to frown

She'd say, "Hey, little feller, don't you cry no more,
Let's go down to the candy store.
You can have your pick from all that you see
Down at The Candy Factory."

Well, the lady at the counter said, "What'll it be?
Two cents each or a nickel for three."
"Well, I've got a dime, so it don't bother me!
Mama, pick me up so I can see!"

Got Mary Janes, coconut drops
Chocolate Chubbies and a lollipop
Zig-Zag, candy corn, please don't stop
Fill my bag clean up to the top

"Hey, little feller, don't you cry no more,
Let's go down to the candy store.
You can have your pick from all that you see
Down at The Candy Factory."

Well, the years went by and now I'm grown
And I've got a little one of my own
If we get missing, you know where we've gone
Back uptown to our home-sweet-home

We got Mary Janes, coconut drops
Chocolate Chubbies and a lollipop
Zig-Zag, candy corn, please don't stop
Fill our bag clean up to the top

"Hey, little feller, don't you cry no more,
Let's go down to the candy store.
You can have your pick from all that you see
Down at The Candy Factory."

So, if you get down and feel forlorn
Head on down to the candy store
Guaranteed to fill your heart with glee
Down at The Candy Factory

Yeah, it's chocolate-covered memories
Down at The Candy Factory

THE LOAD

On a good night, the twelve-string guitar and harp combination sounds like the church organ that I used to hear sometimes during the warm summer months of my childhood. It was in a time before air conditioning, and I reckon the "colored" church across the woods must have opened the windows to keep the ladies from fainting.

We went to church, usually in the morning, and we had a piano, but no organ. We had a choir, too, but it didn't sound like the singing that came from that old church. It seeped through the trees like a hallowed mist, sometimes soft and sweet and other times much louder and intense.

I wanted to go there and hear this music up close, but that wasn't allowed back then. Not really because of any "ism" or bad feelings toward the people. Actually, it was quite the opposite of that, more like a kind of respect.

Sometimes, people have different ways of doing the same thing, and those differences should be respected. I usually ended up "respecting" from the outermost edge of the yard (the one closest to the woods at the end of the road where the little church was).

The Load is a spiritual song from a totally human perspective, the way the Carters or Hank Williams or the Reverend Gary Davis used to do so effectively. It centers around real people, real situations… and real solutions.

The Load

Family's seen better days, that one thing's for sure
Ain't nobody knows you when you're poor
You gather up your dignity, try to make a stand
But things don't always turn out like you plan

Now, Daddy went to prison, eight years ago
He couldn't take the pressure, he buckled from The Load

She comes into the bedroom to kiss 'em all goodnight
She fumbles with the vespers and the light
She glances in the mirror hanging on the wall
Then moves to meet the stranger in the hall

Now, Mama's on the street tonight, strung out on the blow
Her body, once a temple, laid ruined by The Load

A man is in the darkness, a voice is crying low
He struggles with the way that He must go
He knows the deed is needed, and He knows the time is right
He sees the gang approaching in the night

Now, they took Him to the mountain, and the blood began to flow
He paid the debt for everyone, held captive by The Load

Intermission:
The Poetry Corner

VOWEL MOVEMENT

Being a songwriter of sorts, I reckon it's only natural that at some point or another I might fancy writing some poetry. Not expecting to compete with the likes Poe, Dickerson, or Ginsburg, I figure it shouldn't be too difficult a task. A poem is, after all, just song lyrics without the music and should actually be easier to write.

That thought materialized a while back, and I set to the task at the beginning of the week.

Three weeks and two composition books later, I didn't have three lines that I considered good enough to even read myself, much less allow for others. It was disturbing, and although you'd have a hard time getting me to admit it, I felt a dent in the ego that I thought I had long ago locked up in a trunk and slid under my bed.

A few days later, I was out by the deck watching two robins try to stomp each other and had an idea for a song. I went inside, grabbed my journal and began jotting down some thoughts.

In no more than an hour, I had the rough draft of a new song complete. Not one bird was made mention in it, by the way, but it assured me that my ability to at least form sentences and rhyme and word here and there hadn't left me.

I didn't even glance toward poetry again. Being once bitten, I was indeed twice shy and still wasn't convinced that my one experience hadn't been a close call to a demise in songwriting skills.

It did still bother me that I had such an impossible time with it, though. Actually, "interest" is a more appropriate term. Very few things bother me about myself, and if you take that as being vain in any way, you are 180 degrees plumb off about it. I just don't tend to take myself that serious.

I did revisit the thought a bit later. Yep, same deck, no robin smack-down, and the whole thing kinda cleared like a fogged window when the defroster kicks in.

A song with lyrics has one purpose and one purpose only – to be sung. A poem is absolutely the same except the media, or conduit, to its performance is to be read.

I don't approach songwriting with the goal of my lyrics being read. I know they are remembered because people ask and comment about them. But reading, and especially reading out loud, is more akin to acting than singing, and I could never be accused of that.

After figuring the matter out, I did make another attempt at writing a poem, mainly just for fun and to prove that I hadn't been defeated by the rascal.

Here are the results of what is, most likely, my only attempt at writing poetry. You'll have your chance to give an opinion on that at the end.

Vowel Movement

I got struck by lightening today
Didn't hurt much, I'm okay
Not much else to say
Can't feel my legs… HOORAY! HOORAY!

I got hit by a truck today
No harm done, it's safe to say
Truck was green, or was it gray?
Darned if I remember… HOORAY! HOORAY!

I had a heart attack today
Usual kind, usual way
Went towards the light, wanted to stay
Doctor brought me back… HOORAY? HOORAY?

Stuck my head in a vise today
Tightened it up, all the way
Flattened by brain like a serving tray
Feels much better… HOORAY! HOORAY!

I ate a whole mad cow today
Horns and all, it's the only way
Lured him in with a bit of hay
NOW I'M MAD… HOORAY! HOORAY!

I made up this poem today
Wasn't like work, more like play
Ran out of words that end in "ay"
Guess I'll stop… _____! _____!

THE ESSENTIAL
SCOTT GIBSON

WON'T BE TREAD UPON

"I won't be wronged, I won't be insulted, and I won't be laid a hand on. I don't do these things to other people, and I expect the same from them."

– John Wayne, *The Shootist*

Won't Be Tread Upon

You shop for justice in the bargain aisle
And I bite my tongue if I dare to smile
They wouldn't know the truth if it bit 'em
And I just ain't got time to waste anymore

Standin' with my back against the wall
Waitin' for the dominos to fall

I got a name, and I got a face
And I got the right to stand in my space
And I won't be tread upon

You snub your nose at society
And I keep my heart under lock and key
They wouldn't know respect if it bit 'em
And I just ain't got time to waste anymore

Standin' with my back against the wind
Waitin' for the sun to come again

Yeah, and I got a name, and I got a face
And I got the right to stand in my space
And I won't be tread upon

Hey, I got a voice, and I got a brain
And I got eyes, and I ain't insane
And I won't be tread upon

I won't be tread upon
Won't be tread upon

BREAKIN' MY MIND ALL THE TIME

A flashback from the 60's; "break my mind" just kinda stuck with me because of its simplistic way of defining such a complex condition.

A "mind breaker" (not to be confused with the less-intense "mind bender") is a total shutdown of logical comprehension. It's like fifteen-thousand "I don't understand's" rammed into a single paper cylinder and lit with a short fuse.

The who's, what's, and where's seem to change quite often in this tune. Sometimes "I" is indeed "me"... sometimes "you"... and sometimes, someone different altogether. That is the beauty of the abstract approach; it really doesn't change, but it's never really the same.

Beyond that, I'm convinced that a good many of my lyrics are not really for me to understand or interpret. Sometimes when I'm performing certain pieces, I almost feel like I'm intruding on somebody else's business, like I'm reading some other person's mail.

Very odd... very cool... very odd.

Breakin' My Mind All the Time

I used to be the one you came to hear
And even though the point was dull, I'd stick it in your ear
Went away to Neverland, never to grow old
I just came back to tell you
This hand's about to fold

Breakin' my mind all the time
Breakin' my mind all the time
Every time it looks like I'm feeling fine
You start breakin' my mind all the time

You laugh when I ramble on this way
Ain't got no ticket, so how much do I pay?
The questions still to answer, the prophesy is cast
Whatever you plan to do to me
Better do it fast

Breakin' my mind all the time
Breakin' my mind all the time
Every time it looks like I'm feeling fine
You start breakin' my mind all the time

So, I'll leave you with a wish and this prayer
One day you'll look for me, but I won't be there
The shadow's on the window, the writing's on the wall
The things you hold so precious
Don't matter much at all

Breakin' my mind all the time
Breakin' my mind all the time
Every time it looks like I'm feeling fine
You start breakin' my mind all the time

BLUE JAY

In times past, when a marriage was to take place, certain formalities had to be addressed before the actual ceremony could take place.

The first major step was the betrothal. Betrothal involved the establishment of a marriage covenant.

The prospective bridegroom would travel from his father's house to the home of the prospective bride. There, he would negotiate with the father of the young woman to determine the price he must pay for her.

Once the bridegroom paid the price, the marriage covenant was established and the two were considered husband and wife. From that moment on, the bride was declared to be consecrated, or set apart, exclusively for the bridegroom.

After the covenant was established, the bridegroom would leave that house and return to that of his father. There, he would remain separate from his bride for a certain period of time while he prepared accommodations in his father's house to which he could later bring his bride.

The bride, who fully expected her husband to return for her, didn't know the exact time or day of that return. She spent her days in preparation for being the best wife she could be.

Upon his return, the husband would carry his bride back to the bridal chamber in the place he had prepared for them to live. There, they would consummate the marriage and begin their life together as man and wife.

Blue Jay

Blue Jay, how come you took my gal away?
I ain't had no lovin'
Since she's been gone

Payday, I was gonna take her out and say
How much I loved her
And wanted her to be my own

Finally got the nerve to ask her daddy for her hand
Only to discover, she'd left to sing with an emo band

So Blue Jay, won't you bring her back today?
'Cause without my baby, I just can't make it no more

Listen to me, Blue Jay, now don't you turn and fly
If I can't have her back again, I'll lay me down to die

So, Blue Jay, won't you bring her back today?
'Cause without my baby, I just can't make it no more

HEY, DRIVER

So very different now than even a decade ago, yet in many ways the same as they have been for centuries. I'm talking about the folks who haul the freight, the products, and the raw materials that keep us alive and well and entertained and informed… the truck drivers.

A unique sort, if ever there was one. The kind of folks that, unless you are one or live with one, you probably know very little about. They are shrouded in mystery; seen, but seldom encountered outside of the cockpit of those bellowing behemoths that blow us all over the highway as they pass.

Perched high in the skulls of those slithering giants, it's for sure they don't see the world as we "car people" see it. Their limitations and special needs have forced a whole industry to accommodate and cater to them, and that industry is pretty much exclusive to them and not frequented or even known about by us mere "mortals". In many ways, it's like a world within a world, a whole different dimension that can only be seen through the windshield of a semi.

They have a better communication system than the US Army and seem to be able to tell the future when it comes to the traffic jam eight miles ahead or the patrolman behind the next overpass. I do imagine, though, that there are times, especially the times when "late" becomes "early" and the traffic has thinned out, and the chatter on the CB has faded into white noise, that it can be awesomely lonely out there.

Even with all the new technology and communication gizmos, there are surely times when all there is… is a driver alone with his thoughts. Thoughts about home, the wife and kids, and the truck payment that he's bustin' a gut right now to make. Usual kind of stuff… human kind of stuff.

Hey Driver, I feel ya, brother. Keep her steady as she goes, and I'll catch ya on the flip. We need ya, Driver… hang in there.

Hey, Driver

Here's a song for all them drivers
The ones still out there on the road
Your life is measured by the miles that you run
Your worth, measured by the load

The sun comes up in Carolina
But he's two hours down the line
With thoughts of his wife, and his babies, and his life
A-layin' heavy on his mind

So pour down another cup of coffee
And keep her steady as she goes
Your life is measured by the miles that you run
Your worth, measured by the load

Now, it's a wonder he ain't crazy
From all them hours on the road
Sometime' he'd like to fold, but he plays the hand he holds
'Cause drivin's all he knows

You say your daddy taught you drivin'
Just like his daddy taught to him
And you'd like to pass it on, but the way things are goin'
The chance is looking mighty slim

So pour down another cup of coffee
And keep her steady as she goes
Your life is measured by the miles that you run
Your worth, measured by the load

DESIRE IS A FLAME

Desire, pride, envy, and greed.

The source of so much pain and suffering for humanity.

And yet, all so very human.

Desire is a Flame

Desire is a flame, hard to contain
Blow upon the coals, it's out of control
Resting in the ashes of emotion is the notion to refrain
But waiting in the darkness, the monster, rising again

Pride is a pool, gazed into by fools
Perfection to view, it's all about you
Here upon the surface, the reflection, a connection to the brain
Lurking in the deep, the ego, selfish and vain

Envy is a vine, sure to entwine
Allow it grow, choke out your soul
Material discontentment allows a deep resentment to reign
'Till a heart as hard as stone is all that remains

Greed is a snare, step in if you dare
No matter how much, it's never enough
Somewhere in confessing, an obsession with possessions is found
Inviting the bonds of debt to turn around

Watch out, watch out…

LIKE A RIVER

I spent a good portion of my life with the attitude that the "path of least resistance" is always the best approach. Not a path that includes such bothers as confrontations or compromise, but one that avoids them.

Water is like that. It glides through the terrain, spurred upon by the natural force of gravity, and winds around anything that stands in its way.

But years later, I came to realize that some of the obstacles placed in our paths are there for a purpose. To avoid them is to miss the opportunity to better ourselves or enhance our life experiences.

Water is like that as well. Part of the flow does avoid the obstacle and seep around, but another part hangs in there and confronts it. That confrontation is the force that forms those interesting and beautiful water features we all love to explore and photograph. It often erodes away the rock to the point where a huge nugget of pure gold might be exposed for the picking.

Like a River

An old man sits on the back porch
The eyes of wisdom growin' dim
He speaks, but not above a whisper
To the young boy sittin' there with him

"Listen, and I'll give you my secret,
I know you might not understand,"
Then he smiled and said,
"Just remember, when you grow up to be a man…"

"Life is like a river,
Ever-flowin', wild and free.
It starts up high on the mountain,
And journeys down to the sea.
Sometimes it winds through the canyon,
Dashed upon the rocks, so rough and cruel.
But sometimes it flows through the valley
Into a deep and peaceful pool."

I know I'll always remember
Though I live to be a hundr'd three
The words of life, everlasting
And the old man that gave them to me

He said, "Life is like a river,
Ever-flowin', wild and free.
It starts up high on the mountain,
And journeys down to the sea.
Sometimes it winds through the canyon,
Dashed upon the rocks, so rough and cruel.
But sometimes it flows through the valley
Into a deep and peaceful pool."

"Yes, sometimes it flows through the valley
Into a deep and peaceful pool."

BABYLON JAIL

This is one of my absolute favorites to play. Sometimes, when I've nailed the tempo and the harmonica sounds like a circus calliope, a smile carves itself into my face, and I'm reminded exactly why I do this.

Babylon Jail… Billy the Kid meets King Nebuchadnezzar, perhaps?

Too deep for me… Hell, ain't it?

Babylon Jail

I hit town in climbin' gear
Too little sense, too much beer
Got into trouble and wound up here, at the Babylon jail

Got no lawyer to do my deal
Got no circumstance to appeal
Got no evidence to reveal at the Babylon jail

Am I lost? Have I fell? I can't tell…
And they're stokin' up the furnace outside my cell
Pray somebody come and go my bail
Fire and sulfur, it stink like hell at the Babylon jail

Well, Shadrach, Meshach, Abednego
King says, "Bow!" they say, "No!"
Chunk 'em chill'un in a fiery hole at the Babylon jail

Now Old King Neb had him a dream
Dan gonna tell him what it really means
Dew is wet, grass is green, at the Babylon jail

Am I lost? Have I fell? I can't tell…
Oh, and they're stokin' up the furnace outside my cell
Pray somebody come and go my bail
Fire and sulfur, it stink like hell at the Babylon jail

Rich man sittin' at a lovely feast
Lazarus beggin' for the crumbs to eat
Plenty of fire here to cook your meat at the Babylon jail

Now, send a little water if that's okay
Abe said, "Man, there ain't no way!"
Boss says, "Guilty! You must pay!" at the Babylon jail

Am I lost? Have I fell? I can't tell…
Oh, and they're stokin' up the furnace outside my cell
Pray somebody come and go my bail
Fire and sulfur, it stink like hell at the Babylon jail

Yeah, the Babylon jail
Woah, the fire and sulfur, it stink like hell at the Babylon jail
Mmm, at the Babylon jail

SAD TO CRY

I am not a person who handles the level of despair expressed in this piece very well at all. I think I have some sort of inner defense mechanism that blows like a fuse before such an emotional overload as this can enter and permanently damage my circuits.

If it relates to me on any level, it must be some kind of deflection that I dare not look upon in reality.

I'm an optimistic fellow, and what few sips of the bitter wine of depression I have tasted, I've instantly spat out, instinctively recognizing it as the most potent of poisons to my system.

Actually, I believe in my bones that this song was meant for certain people, maybe one person in particular, as some kind of potion meant to soothe an ache that I myself couldn't imagine, much less, endure.

Most times I perform it, I can deliver the goods and lift off before the flack begins to strike my hull. But on occasion, a bit of radioactive medicine seeps into my own soul, and I swear the breath seems to drain right out of me, and I feel my very sanity come into harm's way.

Sounds kinda melodramatic and downright eerie, I know. I'm just telling it like it is.

I will continue to sing this song because it was given to me for that purpose. The comfort I get from it is the hope that whomever it is for will hear it, and in some way, be helped.

Sad to Cry

The sun invades your bedroom
Through the window where the curtains leave a crack
And you pour out of the bed
Feeling like you've been run over by a Mack
As you splash your face with water
Reach up for the towel that's in the rack
You glance into the mirror
But don't recognize the person staring back

And it's too late for sorry
But it's too soon to die
And you're too close to idle back and coast
But you're too sad to cry

You wander down the hall
Hear the clock on the mantle striking ten
Then you glance towards the kitchen
But you just can't find the courage to go in
As you slide down on the sofa
And you can't help thinking how it might've been
And you'd give all that you own
Just to hear the sound of laughter once again

And it's too late for sorry
But it's too soon to die
And you're too close to idle back and coast
But you're too sad to cry

Yes, it's too close to idle back and coast
But you're too sad to cry

BALL AND CHAIN

As the music developed for this work, I continually had problems with the tempo. Now, how could that be possible with only me producing the music? We'll all have to ponder a bit, but it was so, none the less.

I always start with a basic stereo track of vocals and guitar, and many times the recording process ends there. If I do decide that some more instruments will enhance the recorded version of the song, I'll add them accordingly.

I try to stay within certain parameters when recording so as not to over-produce the product too far past what I can recreate live. That's probably silly on my part, because I never play a song the same way twice, anyway. But that's another story.

As I tried to lay down some other guitar lines on the base track, I kept stumbling over the tempo and losing the beat, like Steve Martin in *The Jerk*. It was just that awkward. Rather than stop for the day in a frustrated state of rhythm, I just sat back on the stool and tried to collect myself for another go at it.

As I sat there trying not to think, I started mouthing some kind of meaningless growl, half way between trying to talk with your mouth full and clearing your throat. As I continued, my right hand picked up the action and began to snap its fingers in time, kinda like Tennessee Ernie on *Sixteen Tons*.

I reached over to start the recorder, hoping to just catch the tempo so I could build on it later, but I missed the record button and hit play. That started the playback of the track already put down. Instantly, I realized what the problem was that "had its way" with me for over two hours. The reason I had such a problem saddling up to that tempo wasn't the tempo at all... it was the key the original track was played in.

The "growl" track was a full note lower, and when I sang it down there, I naturally slid into a tempo that was as easy to abide with as a pair of five year old running shoes. I quickly re-recorded the base track in that key, and in no more than half an hour, I had another guitar, bass line, and some harp added. It was almost too easy.

A bit of that "mouthy growl" seeped out near the end of the song, and it never fails to give me a chuckle when I hear it. I also did an extended ending on this song, for no other reason than I was so into the tempo that I just didn't want to stop. It's one of the perks of the job.

Ball and Chain

When I was young, my daddy said, "Son,
I wanna tell you man to man,
Now, listen real close, and I'll tell you somethin'
You might not understand."

"A woman was put here for a sole purpose
To drive a poor man insane.
Don't give your love to no one-time woman,
'Cause love ain't nothin' but a ball and chain."

Ain't nothin' but a ball and chain
Put here to drive a poor man insane
Ain't nothin' but a ball and chain

When I grew up, I finally found
That what my daddy said was true
Now, I can't eat, child, and I can't sleep at night
And it's all because of you

Let me tell you, lover, if I had to do it over
I'd do it all the same
When you love me, baby, I can't move a muscle
'Cause love ain't nothin' but a ball and chain

Ain't nothin' but a ball and chain
Put here to drive a poor man insane
Ain't nothin' but a ball and chain

HEY JOHNNY, GIT YER GUN

Back in elementary school, every so often, the music teacher would come around to our classroom and give us a lesson in music appreciation. Now, our regular teachers could hold their own when it came to leading a song here and there, but this lady was special, and her efforts made an impression on me that lingers to this day. Much of my curiosity and interest in the background behind a song came from those early lessons.

Stories about early settlers and the Cumberland Gap, drummer boys in the way between the states, and barge drivers on the Eerie Canal kept this ol' boy glued to the edge of his seat and eager to chime in when it was time to sing.

I do, on occasion, and with great pleasure, visit my daughter's classroom to share a bit of folk music with them. I tell them the stories behind some of my topical songs like *Lexitown*, *The Watcher*, and "The Fire Truck Song". As I sing to them, I can see that same kind of wonder and interest in them that I remember having when the music teacher came around. That settles in good with me.

So, here's to all the teachers out there, especially the ones who recognize that a simple song can break down barriers and set a child's feet on a good path just as surely as any arithmetic test or reading circle.

Hey Johnny is meant to sound like a period piece, but the language and theme is not shackled by something as impotent as time. No force on Earth seems to be able to curb mankind's seemingly inherent urge to make war on itself. And until one comes along, the words of this song will apply.

Hey Johnny, Git Yer Gun

Hey Johnny, git yer gun, that silver, shiny one
Load it up with powder and with ball
Come out into the street, your brother, there to meet
Your country is giving you the call

You are just a lad, but this situation's bad
The enemy is just beyond the hill
Tell Maw and Paw goodbye, for today you're bound to die
We didn't think the threat was so real

We should have taken heed when they done that bloody deed
We should have sounded trumpets to attack
What turned into a sport for the lawyers and the courts
Has now returned to stab us in the back

They said the cause was just, so we offered up our trust
Unto the mighty architects of war
They didn't tell us then they'd be comin' 'round again
Now we must do battle like before

Come the light of dawn, we'll be no more than pawns
Among the knights and bishops on the board
An evening's warming fire will become a funeral pyre
For those of us cut down by the hoard

We sing an ancient song, as we go marching on
Of soldiers and of battles long ago
I hope they tell it true when they sing of me and you
So all our sons and daughters will know

JIHAD BLUES

The most common word used to describe my sense of humor is… *warped*! I can't help it. I was born that way.

An example of this "warpedness" would be to replace a vicious and sinister subject, such as a suicide bomber, with one that resembles Don Knott's Barney Fife.

Can you just imagine?

Hmm… it seems I'm not the only one with a sense of humor that's a few degrees plumb off.

My apologies to anyone offended by this song. The objective was not to offend, but to find some common, human emotion that might lead to an attitude change.

Most people would rather be shot at than laughed at.

It's worth a try, anyway.

Jihad Blues

Call me Ishmeal, but not too loud
Don't want to stand out too much in a crowd
My head is buzzin' and my finger's ready to press
I feel the need to lay it down
But I don't know east from west

Sixteen candles upon my breast
Sewn up into a bullet-proof vest
Call for the police, but the police ain't got a clue
I feel the need to connect
But I don't know green or blue

Write down my name, write it on a stone
Tell all the women there to weep and moan
Stoke up the bonfires, call out the CNN
I feel the need to end it all
But I just can't begin

I have a dream, same one each night
I hear the gunfire, but I can't find the fight
Everywhere around me, I see infidels and Jews
I feel the need to express
But I just can't light the fuse

It ain't no use, I can't go through
With this evil thing I'm supposed to do
There goes my palace, there go my virgin brides
I feel the need to Jihad
But I just can't suicide

TIME, TIME, TIME

I wrote this song during a time when I was experimenting with over-dubbing some other instruments here and there on some of the tracks. Adding other instruments is natural to me, but I'm careful not to produce any signature sounds or riffs that I can't reproduce live.

This has always been the prime directive in my recording efforts – to keep it real. On this particular track, however, I kinda let myself go and added two more guitars, some bass, a bit of percussion, and a drone sound produced with my sour-string tenor guitar in an open tuning.

I wasn't too aware of the big picture as I recorded each layer; I didn't do a full playback until I was ready to work on the master mix. The master mix is basically the blending of each recorded track into the final stereo mix. I set the levels fairly even and hit the play button to begin the process. The music rolled out of the monitors and immediately took me down some kind of surreal rabbit hole and into a place I didn't imagine I could ever go.

This music, which is so centered and focused on time, sounded like a clock. More than that, as I sat between and facing the speakers, it sounded like I was inside that clock. The different accents and rhythms of the guitars, the percussion, the drone sound... all came together in a way that mimicked the sound of the many different wheels and cogs and chimes that is a clock.

Synchronicity is one of those wonderful terms that sounds cool when dropped in a smart conversation, but to witness it actually happening is straight-up awesome. The marriage of music to lyric to theme is not uncommon. It is, on one hand, a difficult and very high form of art achieved only by the most masterful artists; on the other, a common magician's trick used in advertising to sell soap or beer.

I would be overjoyed to be able to take full credit for either, but alas, the only credit I can manage is the fact that I wrote and produced it. I guess I'll just have to be content with that.

My consolation… the listeners who tell me that *Time* conjures up the most emotion in them and is their favorite song of all I have written.

Time, Time, Time

One man counts his money, another man counts his woes
One man feeds his children, the other feeds his nose
One man shops designer stores in big fancy malls
Another man shops the bargain stores or he don't shop at all

But time... you can't buy it
Time, time, time... only spend it

One man lives in the city, another man on the farm
One man cold and hungry, the other full and warm
One man sleeps at the Hilton in the presidential suite
While another man sleeps in a cardboard box out there in the street

But time... you can't buy it
Time, time, time... only spend it

One many owns the factory, another man works the dock
One man gets a salary, the other punch the clock
One man sells that factory and retires at thirty-nine
Another man stands for hours in the unemployment line

But time... you can't buy it
Time, time, time... only spend it

One man sees a doctor, he's rich enough to pay
Another man lets the gov'ment pay his bill for free
One man buys insurance to cover him when he's ill
Another man can't do nothin' 'cept write himself a will

But time... you can't buy it
Time, time, time... only spend it

One man puts his faith in God, another man in himself
One man reads the scripture, another holistic health
One thing true of every man, and there can be no doubt
No matter how you spend your time, one day it will run out

But time… you can't buy it
Time, time, time… only spend it

THERE ONCE WAS A MAN

Purpose is a mighty lord when applied to the life of a human being.

Given the choice, I reckon most folks would prefer a life with purpose over one without. But what constitutes a purpose, and why do humans seem to want it in their lives?

Is it predestined and bound to happen, no matter what?

Is it left entirely to the individual to find and fulfill?

Does it span a whole lifetime, or does it last no longer or consist of no more than a single, solitary act or event?

Does a man who lives his entire life working and supporting a family exhibit less purpose than another man who devotes his life to finding the cure for cancer?

On the surface, the latter case might seem to give evidence of a more purposeful life. However, one little tweak, one short span of time, one single, myopic event, could change everything. Imagine that the second man never finds that cure, but years later, he mentors a young scientist who eventually does. This young scientist turns out to be the second child of the working father in the first story plot.

I suppose the moral to all of this is that no matter who you are or what you do in life, we all have to agree that we're part of some greater, collective purpose. Our lives, no matter how insignificant they may seem or appear, are, in fact, important and necessary.

Every deed, every action, every word, every gesture that constitutes our life *does* affect the whole of humanity, and that contribution is as immortal as time itself.

This is a good thing to remember when the temptation to look down on another person rears up. It's much harder to feel superior to someone "less" than yourself if you consider he, or his children, or their children, may indeed have a purpose in life that will one day impact that of your own in a mighty way.

Oh, the song? Here ya go...

JesusChristGandhiKennedyPaulBrownLennonJohntheBaptistLincolnKing

There Once Was a Man

There once was a man, and he spoke to the people
And traveled about through the land
And he spoke about love, and he spoke forgiveness
And things that would benefit man

But they cut him down on the streets of Jerusalem
And they cut him down on the streets of Rome
And they cut him down on the banks of the Jordan
And the people… just talked to a wall

There once was a man, and he spoke to the people
And traveled about through the land
And he spoke about love, and he spoke of freedom
And things that would benefit man

But they cut him down on the streets of Concord
And they shot him down in the District of Columbia
And they shot him down on the streets of New Deli
And the people… stood, bouncin' a ball

There once was a man, and he spoke to the people
And traveled about through the land
And he spoke about love, and he spoke equality
And things that would benefit man

But they shot him down on the streets of Dallas
And they shot him down on the streets of Memphis
And they shot him down on the streets of Manhattan
And the people… took off to the mall

HAIL, OCEANIA

When I was very young, one of my favorite LP's was a collection of sea shanties sung by some character who called himself Capt'n Bill. It was a fabulous record with songs like *Blow the Man Down*, *Sloop John B*, and *What Shall We Do With a Drunken* (I think it used "silly") *Sailor?*, backed by flutes and squeezeboxes and all kinds of cool-sounding gear. I used to listen to it for hours on end and could actually transcend the confines of my little house on the dirt road and sail away with Capt'n Bill to exotic ports of call.

See, that's how powerful music, especially folk music, is. It has that ability, that omnipotence. I consciously wanted to tap into that as I began to write, and this is as close as I've come yet.

Where is the city or country of Oceania? Why, it's in the center of the continent of Europa, of course. With a land mass "bridge" above and below it that borders other lands.

Could we in the US ever fall victim to "her" fate?

Some may say we already have.

Hail, Oceania

Gather 'round, all you sons and you daughters
Listen to what I will say
I'll tell you a tale of a beautiful city
And the fate that would meet her one day

She sits like a queen in her ivory tower
Surrounded by oceans of blue
With a bridge to the north, and a bridge to the south
And subjects both loyal and true

Hail, Oceania, the pride of Europa
The light in the darkness, the land of the free
Mother to orphans, the bride of the righteous
Long may you shine for the whole world to see

In the way of the merchant, there's no one to challenge
All of her storehouses, full
Her factories working, her people to prosper
Her standard in trade is the rule

She sets the example for honor and justice
Her bell of freedom does ring
All of the people, of all of the nations
Lift up their voices to sing

Hail, Oceania, the pride of Europa
The light in the darkness, the land of the free
Mother to orphans, the bride of the righteous
Long may you shine for the whole world to see

Then one day a ship from a faraway country
Into her port, it did sail
And she opened her arms to the wandering sailors
Cast out by tyranny's gale

But the cowards betrayed her, and set out to slay her
By fear and hate they were bound
Their arrows did fly, and light up the sky
And burned her down to the ground

Hail, Oceania, the pride of Europa
The light in the darkness, the land of the free
Mother to orphans, the bride of the righteous
Long may you shine for the whole world to see

Hail, Oceania, the pride of Europa
The light in the darkness, the land of the free
Mother to orphans, the bride of the righteous
Never to shine for the whole world to see

TABLE OF THE LORD

It's so easy – as we scurry about the business of being who we are – to pass by that tattered, scraggly-looking fellow standing over near the alley. And if we notice at all, that glance often quickly turns into disgust or fear or utter disdain for someone who would let themselves get to that status of life.

I mean, why don't they get a job and clean themselves up, or at least stay out of the public where decent people don't have to see them and parents don't have to explain them to their kids? Why are they there? Who are they? Do they not have family to help look after them? Is there no one they can turn to for a decent coat to keep the wind out, or a hot meal, or a bed somewhere off the street?

There is actually someone who can provide these things. But sadly, that someone just passes him by and never notices him. Or if they notice at all, that glance quickly turns into disgust or fear or utter disdain and causes the would-be helper to scurry away, preoccupied with the business of being who they are.

Who is that tattered, scraggly, homeless, hungry fellow? It's only me, if not for the grace of the Good Lord. The same Lord that will one day preside as groom over a banquet table fit for Himself and His bride.

Where is that tattered, scraggly, homeless, and hungry fellow? First chair to the left, the one with the clean, white coat and golden rings, resting his head on the Master's bosom.

Where is the only one who could have given the poor man a bit of comfort, but failed to do so? It seems there was no place for him at this table.

Table of the Lord

I ain't nobody, pay me no mind
Who am I to tell you how to live your life?
I'm just a vessel of broken clay
Nothin' to judge you in what I say

But even a blind man can see the light
And even a thief can do what's right
And even a leper can lift up his eyes and say,
"When the sky splits with lightning,
And the plows are beat into swords,
And the sun turns black as midnight,
I want to be at the table of the Lord."

I ain't nothin' special, pay me no heed
Just another fool, just another weed
Down in the valley, covered in mud
Even a weed gains strength from the sun

But even a junkie can see the light
And even a politician can do what's right
And even a murderer can lift up his eyes and say,
"When the sky splits with lightning,
And the plows are beat into swords,
And the sun turns black as midnight,
I want to be at the table of the Lord.

…At the table of the Lord.
…Table of the Lord."

"Scott-isms", Wisdom, and Woe

A NOTE ON "SCOTT-ISMS"
By Lindsay Gibson Goins

Throughout his life, my dad was known for using ambiguous metaphors and quirky analogies. He often presented me with advice by telling an elaborate story with a particularly subjective moral that I'd have to ponder for a few days in order to determine what he was trying to teach me.

Dad had a way of bringing a subtle, yet unforgettable dissonance to the forefront of my mind whenever he used this special form of symbolism to communicate ideas. It was like hearing an electric fence buzzing in my mind – a constant reminder that I needed to put on my thinking cap and address the real issue at hand. Yep, he definitely had a talent for making people rack their brains.

Many friends and family members have told me that my dad chose his words wisely and meant everything he said. He was a master wordsmith, not only in lyrical form, but in casual conversation. After some time, many folks began referring to his quick-witted remarks as "Scott-isms" because of the parable-like nature of his reflections about the world around him.

So, I suppose the term "Scott-ism" is simply a word to describe a witticism or euphemism directly from the warped mind of the one and only Scott Gibson.

A classic "Scott-ism" could definitely be described as "not heavy, just awkward" because you'd find yourself reciting the words over and over, puzzled and perplexed, yet quite certain at the same time. *Was that an insult or a compliment? Did he just... oh! He must be really liberal... no, definitely conservative. What planet did this guy just land from? Is he for real? Am I offended, or just completely inspired?*

Usually my dad's goal was to make you feel just awkward and uncomfortable enough to step out of your comfort zone and do something about it… whatever "it" may have been.

Of course, there were times when "Scott-isms" weren't really "-isms" at all. Sometimes he said exactly what needed to be said, requiring no additional thought, because what he had to say was simply too important to be misconstrued or left up to interpretation.

Other times, "Scott-isms" were fairly simple to understand on the surface, but carried a familiar, yet thought-provoking after-shock.

My dad amused himself with social media. He enjoyed posting some of his "Scott-isms" on Facebook for friends to mull over. Some of his messages were obvious, while others required more effort.

Within this section, I've included a collection of "Scott-isms". Some were Facebook posts, while others are remarks that friends and family members have recalled.

I've also incorporated an assortment of poetry, prose, song lyrics, and journal entries. Some of the lyrics belong to compositions that were never recorded; some were recorded but have not been found. Several of the writings to follow date back to the 70's, while others are more recent. Some of my favorites were hand-written in the journal that I gave him for Father's Day a few years ago (pictured on the cover of this book along with his harmonica).

To say that I've had the time of my life going through my dad's notebooks and old Facebook posts is an understatement. Reading his thoughts and imagining his raspy, story-teller voice filling my ears with truth has helped me feel closer to him and develop a deeper understanding of just how incredible he was.

I hope you will enjoy this trip into his mind, just as I have.

When you feel without fingers
When you laugh without lips
When you see without looking
When you dance without hips.

When you give even more
When you've got nothing left
When you live and die
In the very same breath.

◇

"There is nothing more restricting than something customized just for you."

"Somewhere along the road, politics took the place of morality in our culture. It did so by offering us a deal that morality couldn't match... the ability to be knowingly wrong, yet politically correct."

◇

The thing about war is that once it begins,
the crueler you wage it, the quicker it ends.
To force one to fight is a terrible sin;
to force one to peace is far worse, again.
Let me die in my footsteps
before I go down under the ground.

I will not go down under the ground
'cause somebody tells me that death's comin' 'round.
And I will not lay myself down to die.
Let me go to my grave with my head held high;
let me die in my footsteps
before I go down under the ground.

You gotta be sharp. Sharp enough so that every ounce of force applied renders a positive, slicing result. No drag, no waste.

You gotta be straight. Straighter than straight. The slightest curve or bend is pure resistance and failure.

You gotta be strong. However strong necessary to maintain your straightness under pressure and drive your edge home and beyond.

You gotta follow through. Dig deep inside and find the courage to act with full confidence. Deem the challenge won, with only a few mere details to handle before checking it off the list.

Do this, and no steel can hold you, no cord can bind you, no stone or bog hinder you, no voice condemn you. You have won before the challenge ever begins. You will survive because there is no other possibility. You are, because you are, and were, and shall ever be. Rise now, take your place, but only for as long as it takes to reckon your next place.
            Then, rise again, forever.

"We seem to place much importance and value on the views we reason and hold. Truth is, most of them are adopted and not reasoned at all, and they hold us more than we hold them."

"Progress cannot be measured when the past is forgotten."

"When all else fails, let's just throw it up against the wall and see if it sticks."

"I have a left eye and a right eye, and neither one a blind eye. This is a condition I like to refer as *Politically Challenged.*"

If I was hungry,
would you feed me?
If I was blind,
would you take me by the hand
and never lead me astray?
If I was helpless,
would you save me?
If I was useless,
torn,
and frayed
around the edges,
would you throw me away,
or mend me
to shape again?

◇

Today we cherish, tomorrow we dust,
Once we did polish, now we let rust.

Once the high mantle, the place it did earn,
Now the dark attic of little concern.

One man's junk, another man's treasure,
Fickle the difference when man is the measure.

◇

First times are wonderful, but rarely best.
First words are usually worthless.
First kisses are painfully awkward,
and last kisses awkwardly painful.
First loves are made of silk.
First impressions are made of steel.
First times can be last times, if they last.

When I look in the faces of people around me,
I seem to see right through to their minds.
And the hurt, and the greed, and the fears that I find there?
It makes me wish I was blind.

When I hear a man call me his brother,
And seal it with blood, sweat, and tears,
And somebody tells me about the put-downs he dealt me?
I wish that I didn't have ears.

God, how it hurts me deep inside;
It torments my very soul.
I look to the sky for some kind of warmth,
But all that I feel is infinite cold.
Sometimes I wish I was dead.

When I look down to see the tears of the children
Whose lives are all mangled and torn,
I can't help but feel that I'm part of the reason,
And I wish I that I'd never been born.

◇

"It doesn't matter if you call yourself a 'latitude' or a 'longitude'. If you don't use both perspectives to navigate, you'll end up going in circles, never quite sure of where you are."

"The most liberating and intellectually stimulating words we can ever speak is the simple phrase… *I am wrong.* A simple admission of what we all know to be true, yet struggle so hard to avoid and deny. It is, perhaps, the most intelligent thing we could ever utter, the most truthful view we could ever hold, and the most 'right' we may ever be."

"Our job as artists is to hold up a mirror to what we see around us."

A small boy sits on an old park bench,
watching the others play.
His body yearns to join them,
but his mind is far away.
They call to him, "Come with us,"
but the voices aren't clear.
"Tomorrow I'll run and play," says he,
"but today I'll just sit here."

A young man sits on an old park bench,
with his bride-to-be.
They plan to live together
and raise a family.
She softly says, "Come love me,"
but his mind is full of fear.
"Tomorrow we'll be in love," says he,
"but today I'll just sit here."

An old man sits on an old park bench,
his features old and worn.
His life is nearly over,
but he does not seem to mourn.
Life is a gift that we all receive,
and we should hold it dear.
Tomorrow I'll play, and love, and live,
but today I'll just sit here.

◇

"If you know the answers to the questions people ask, they call you a genius. If you know the answers to the questions people would rather not ask, they call you an idiot. The genius is no more intelligent or knowledgeable than the idiot, but he does usually get invited to parties."

"It isn't difficult at all to imagine a world without the things you disagree with or object to. The real trick to dealing with reality is to imagine a better world in spite of these things. Dreamer? I think not. Realist, perhaps. But ya gotta start somewhere, or not at all. I'll play the *Imagine* Game your way if you'll play it mine. Or we can just stand on each side of the ditch and call each other names. It's beginning to matter less and less to me."

"Less is more, none is all, 'we' a bridge, 'I' a wall."

◇

Life is like a jigsaw puzzle – every day a piece;
face down on the table, given, lived, then placed.

There are no good or bad ones – none to toss away;
none more or less important; it's all in how they're laid.

Every day can't be a "corner piece" or recognizable bit;
some will be contrary and will not seem to fit.

But fit they will – they must, you see, together right and neat;
the game begins with pieces; the picture began complete.

◇

Sleep sweetly in
your humble graves.
Sleep, martyrs of
a fallen cause.

For lo, a marble
column caves.
The pilgrim here
to pause.

111

Handle Me With Care

Been beat up and battered 'round
Been set up and been shot down
You're the best thing I've ever found
Handle me with care.

Reputations changeable
Situations tolerable
Baby, you're adorable
Handle me with care.

Been stuck in airports, terrorized
Sent to meetings, hypnotized
Overexposed, commercialized
Handle me with care.

Been fobbed-off and I've been fooled
I've been robbed and ridiculed
In daycare centers and night schools
Handle me with care.

I've been uptight and made a mess
And I'll clean it up myself, I guess
Oh, the sweet smell of success
Handle me with care.

"I can only speak for myself, but I've never expected the world to accept me for who I am – only that I be free to be who I am regardless of being accepted."

"The quickest way to end an argument is to attempt to expose your opponent's lack of understanding by admitting to your own."

"The power of our own individuality is only amplified by discovering and embracing the power of community."

"If you're taking a stand and it doesn't cost you something, you're really only taking a sit."

"The only way to control human nature is to act like you can and know that you can't."

"Can't decide what suits me best… less of more, or more of less."

◇

Beware, my child, if your only comfort is the darkness
If being completely vulnerable is your only defense
If recoil your only reaction
If every sound a threat
If every sliver of light an offense
If every brush or bump total destruction
Open your eyes
Do not allow the darkness to define their usefulness
The light will come and you must be ready
It will hurt
The pain is the assurance
The pain is the proof
Your first reaction will be to close your eyes
And return to the darkness
But it won't work
The image seen will reform in your mind and remain
You have become aware
You know the truth
You can no longer find comfort in oblivion
The darkness is no longer a refuge
In the darkness there is no reason to hide
In the light, there is no place.

American Dream, Bye-Bye

Standing out on the asphalt vein
I hear the sound of a sad refrain
Something 'bout "amber waves of grain"
Then it fades away again… to silence.

Man walks by with a plastic bag
Printed on it, a US flag
Out of it he pulls a rag
On that rag, a tag… "Made in China".

Heathen raging, the people dream
Corporation liars scheme
Fueled by the lust of greed
And on the poor they feed… like vultures.

All you need is in this pill
Health will surely make you ill
Better get yourself a will
No matter how you feel… you're still dying.

History books, the how and why
Once were truth, but now are lies
When you see through two left eyes
That teach you to despise… where you came from.

Knowledge surely does abound
Common sense is not around
Techno-science to astound
Doesn't stop the sound… of suffering.

Woe to them that do decree
And make the law for you and me
Cursed with lies and deceit
Leaving only grief... for the people.

   While teachers teach, the masters choose
   While preachers preach, the church eludes
   While poets rhyme, the news construes
   What we have to lose... is our freedom.

      Look into the crystal ball
      Fire and glass will end it all
      Wash it down with alcohol
      'Till you hit the wall... of addiction.

Build your house with criminal hire
Surround it with a razor wire
Those who pass it do admire
The brilliance of the fire... that consumes it.

   Is this pain perpetual?
   Is this wound incurable?
   Pour into the crucible
   Pour until it's full... of repentance.

      Heed the writing on the wall
      Heed it now, before we fall
      Force the evil to withdraw
      With a mighty call... for deliverance.

Rise

Rise, rise and then,
Fly, fly again.
Freedom, take to the sky.
Rise, rise and fly.

The mighty oak may bend against the wind,
But in the morning, rise to greet the sun again.

So rise, rise and then,
Fly, fly again.
Freedom, take to the sky.
Rise, rise and fly,
Rise, and fly.

"America stands boldly on a marble platform holding out Equal Opportunity with both hands… with just a bit of Equal Outcome tucked into her bra, just in case."

"Too many out there say 'I love you' speaking more in terms of tennis than of endearment."

"The idea that in a free society one can be free *to* and another free *from* is simply impossible to understand. What is society but an attempt to defy logic?"

"A bridge is but a toppled wall… pushed against, and made to fall."

"The one thing required to see the good in the world is to know what good is when you see it."

"I'm not fighting cancer. I'm just living."

Light the candle
Break the seal
Spin the wheel

Call your physic
Pop a pill
Spin the wheel

Find a dealer
Make a deal
Spin the wheel

Load your pistol
Shoot to kill
Spin the wheel.

Just expose it
Don't conceal it
Spin the wheel

Keep it natural
Keep it real
Spin the wheel

Push the button
Drink your fill
Spin the wheel

Eat the apple
Toss the peel
Spin the wheel.

Heaven, Come

Jenny has a red balloon tied with a string
to the little wooden stand beside her bed.
Sometimes, late at night, when he comes in,
she stares at it – pretends it is the sun.
Heaven, come.

Billy looks just like his dad, so his Mama says,
like the picture on the wall above the flag.
But he ain't like the other kids at all;
he don't think playing "soldier" is much fun.
Heaven, come.

Bobby used to have it all, or so it seemed.
A wife and kids, a house on Apple Way;
now, somewhere in a motel across town,
he sits there with a bottle and a gun.
Heaven, come.

"To me, any song lyric that doesn't make the listener uncomfortable in some way ain't worth the spit it takes to sing it."

"Every deception began as an undeniable fact."

"Forget about life for a while… now subtract 4… that's what my music is all about."

"Odd how the words 'we're better than that' always come *after* being shown that we indeed aren't."

"No decision made fully and completely in the name of love is ever a wrong decision."

"Odd how any attempt I make toward normality ends up in complete frustration. Even more odd is how very much that pleases me."

"The reason human beings can't learn to love each other is that we begin trying nine months too late and give up trying twenty years too soon."

"If you want to find out how much things have changed, just play along. If you want to find out how little things have changed, just act up."

"Happiness is just too fickle a critter to be on the top of my 'to be' list. I put my money on contentment. Happiness is sugar; contentment, carbs – and I'm in it for the long run."

"Yes, it's true… I *do* seem to have a lot of friends made up of all types and kinds of people. It probably has something to do with not having 'agreeing with me' as a condition for being my friend."

◇

Choosing Sides

Folks are always asking me which side I'm on – with whom do I stand? It never fails to take me back a bit and question my own effectiveness in presenting clear evidence in my life and music. I reckon some clarification is needful, although certainly not due.

I stand with the working guys and gals – the ones who get up and go to work wherever they can, knowing fully that the best that will come from it will only see their families through another day. I am for the ones who believe getting down on their knees on occasion somehow helps them do it.

I am for the ones who teach their children the truth, convenient or not, and allow them to form their own views and tools to navigate life.

I am for the ones who can, and do, take a single moment of joy and make a whole joyful day out of it. I hope that some of that will rub off on me.

I'm for the ones who place fairness and equality above their own gain, and use the one true definition of the terms as their standard.

In short, I seriously doubt I fit on either side of those who seem so eager to place me. That being the case, I'm sure it will not suffice. I hereby give my permission for them to act on their own behalf and put me where they feel I fit.

Friend or foe, I don't care. If you like, give me a t-shirt, issue me a badge. Gotta warn ya, though – if at any time "our" side takes a stand that conflicts with the well-being of those mentioned above, uses or abuses them, attempts to mock or vilify them, I simply won't be there when the next roll is called.

I won't be hard to find should anyone care to give my enlistment another shot. Just find the folks mentioned above and look around for a loud-mouthed guitar picker wearing a funny hat.

◇

"It's simple, really. I'm a liberal when driving and a conservative when a passenger. Next question…"

"No matter how sweet the dish prepared or recipe tried and tested, it all becomes quite vile and sour… once eaten and digested."

"All things considered, you have more in common with your least agreeable neighbor than you have with the most agreeable outsider."

120

A Word on Negativity

It must be tough on the folks who insist on avoiding anything negative in their lives.

I mean, they can't drive their automobile because they've unhooked the cable to the negative post on their battery, can't receive any negative results on medical tests, can't use negative numbers when doing math, and can't have film developed.

The plus side is that they never have to be around negative people who disagree with them and say sad stuff.

However, considering we are all made of atoms, and atoms consist of both positive *and* negative components, they really can't be around anybody or anything, including themselves.

Must be tough.

◇

Well, I don't know where I came from;
don't know where I'm bound.
But I do know that I love you
more than anyone I've found

But it's too soon for knowing,
and it's too late to flee,
and it's too hard to understand
the peace you give to me.

◇

"Odd how often an 'open' mind is accompanied by closed eyes, plugged ears, and humming lips."

Spare Change

Say you want an end to war and violence? Say you want peace and understanding and empathy? Say you want to curb greed and promote brotherhood; empty prisons and alleviate crime? That's a tall order, but there is one key step that when taken, will surely set the stage for filling it.

We as a species must redefine our value of life – any life, in any creature, and at any stage. Our problem, which in turn manifests itself in many areas and ways, is simply that we do not value life as we should, nor teach our children to. Change that, and everything changes. Ignore that, and nothing changes.

◇

The Wind Chime

Consider the wind chime. Those hanging mobiles of metal tubes and string and weights, fashioned to clang against each other when the wind gusts and blows through it. Not so much the fancy ones you buy at high-end import shops with pitch-tuned copper tubes and uniformly stamped weights, but the homemade kind made of hastily painted, inconsistent junk that just happened to be lying around in a state between usefulness.

It does make music, but not in the traditional way like a musical instrument when played or some musical device when wound. It's more of an indicator or gauge that sings of the changing direction and velocity of the wind that inspires it. It reflects that inspiration, and in fact, is quite silent without it.

It could be said that the collective vibrations and attitudes of people are like the wind. Sometimes subtle and indistinguishable amid other distractions, and sometimes very distinct, even violent, but always a true indicator of things that are and of things to come.

I see myself as a wind chime, fashioned to function more as an indicator than instrument, and I see the world around me as the wind – the inspiration, the motivator, the energy. Sometimes it's kinda lonely and difficult when the distractions reign and have their way.

Sometimes hard to keep clanging away when no one seems to notice or care about such things. But then there are times when it is fulfilling to the utmost.

Those times when the distractions fade into each other, leaving just enough silence for the tinkling chime to be heard. The times when the curious get up and move outside for a closer listen, then on to an understanding of what a wind chime is and does, then a glance into the heavens while poking a wet finger into the sky to say, "The wind is picking up and changing direction. Might be a storm on the way. Might need to close the shutters and get out the candles." The wind chime is validated then, fulfilled and content to be what it is; its song and purpose is finally realized and appreciated.

◇

"By far, the greatest hindrance to our pursuit of happiness is our obsession with providing evidence that we have already found it."

"I'd much rather not know what I'm doing, than not know what I've done."

"Hard to lose faith in purpose when every way you turn you step in a huge pile of proof."

"I don't recall anyone ever telling me to 'get over it' and finishing the statement with 'like I did'."

E is for Empathy

Empathy as a means of understanding is highly overrated. Not ineffective, just overrated. We can indeed walk a mile in our brother's shoes, but we can not "be" our brother – know all about him from the experience, base all logic on it. It is quite impossible.

Does that mean empathy is useless as a tool of understanding? Of course not. It is probably the most effective tool, but it can be a major cause of misunderstanding if not used properly or used in conjunction with a previously held bias.

We empathize in an attempt to understand – to answer questions… but the data will always be incomplete and not something our brains recognize as firm footing from which to draw conclusions.

However, "no conclusion" or "some understanding" don't work as a bridge between what we find and what we hope to find (or were *told* we would find). Our brains will, if asked, fill in those gaps with what seem like perfectly good mental stepping stones.

In short, we can't get what we want, but our brains will give us what we need. We can, if we so desire, justify anything and everything if enough Synthetic Blend Empathy is applied.

Used properly, empathy says, "I'm sorry for your loss". Used improperly, it says, "I know exactly how you feel". Both statements may be sincere, but only one can be trusted. Only one is a real basis for understanding.

Empathy is a mind thing – so is imagination. The more imagination it takes, the less empathetic it becomes. I say this in the spirit of real understanding… something much needed these days. But not some painted, Styrofoam version of it. That will not hold up and will crumble when weight is applied.

"The only things that bring people together are a common woe or a common truth."

"The practice of associating yourself with only those who share your particular views will eventually place you solely in the company of the only one who does."

"You don't have to force someone to change their view if you are skilled enough to compel them to change their behavior."

"Bricks and mortar, concrete and steel – given to us all. Now to reckon what to build… a bridge or a wall?"

"I reckon it a good move to think *inside* the box as well."

◇

A Vision Statement

I preface these comments by saying that I blame no one particular person, group, or those who seem to control and motivate them for either creating or perpetuating the problem. I *do* blame every citizen of Davidson County and place my name at the top of the list. This is perhaps an attempt to lower, if not remove, my name from the list.

There is a verse in the Bible that reads, "My people perish for lack of vision," and no alignment of words better defines the problem we are experiencing here. We seem unable to identify, address, and correct any of the problems that work to continuously keep us down and stuck in a social and economic rut.

I believe it's because we fail to see that we are indeed stuck; we don't see the rut, or even the mud as it slings past us. We have a lack of vision because any visible sign of a problem is rendered invisible by those we elect and appoint to lead us.

We choose, among ourselves, those most able to hide the truth from us and our responsibility to it. We do this because the responsibility might distract us from our comfort and shock us from our complacency – something we seem to desire more than anything and pursue with all our passion and effort.

The truth is that we are plagued by the very same problems every other community is plagued with. We have the very same issues and disagreements, the very same hinderances and afflictions that we see each day in the news. However, we are so adamant to deny the truth that we sacrifice any hope of solving or ending these problems by insisting they be hidden from us... made invisible.

We see the homeless lying about in New York City, but see little or none of the homeless who "live" right here in Davidson County.

We see animals being abused and inhumanly killed on the web, yet see little about the many identical cases happening right here.

Gang violence, drug abuse, child abuse – on and on down the list of terrible and tragic things, but none for us, none here to shock and motivate us to do something.

No jobs, no future for our young people, no hope of advancement or progress – a village drying up on the vine, but kept in bloom by whatever artificial means necessary to retain the semblance of prosperity and peace.

We don't think we have a homelessness problem because the problem has been rendered invisible by pushing it back a few blocks out of our vision.

We think we have no problem with irresponsible animal owners because the results of their irresponsibility are carted off for someone else to deal with.

We think we have no problem with gangs or drugs or child abuse because it is kept contained (for now) in the areas where it is most prevalent.

The problem with this type of remedy is that it always fails; no different than a leaky pipe or worn car tire, pretending the problem doesn't exist only compounds the problem and guarantees more and greater problems down the road.

Probably no clearer example of an issue being made "invisible" rather than addressed is the current controversy over symbols of our alignment with the South during the war between the states. There really is but one official symbol of that in Lexington – the monument honoring those who died in the war which stands in the square.

There are indeed many different views and attitudes that can be taken from the gesture. . . many different opinions of its purpose and possible effects. But the whole point of a society – in fact, the very condition of its existence and continuance – lies in the ability of the people who form it to reconcile these differences for the good of all. To use the tools of communication face to face for the most pure and natural of reasons. To practice understanding in its most basic and effectual form. That is how things are made better.

Not by avoidance, but by civil, passionate dialog between people with "skin in the game". There are truths and lessons in all views, and the object is to render them down into one common view and lesson. What seems to have happened is another attempt to make the problem invisible and avoid the hard work of solving it. How do you make a huge statue sitting right in front of everyone invisible? You simply plant a few trees and forget to trim them back away from the subject.

"The key to keeping your faith in humanity is to base it on reality and not fantasy."

The Write Path

I am who I am, I do what I do. I make no apologies for it or attempt to explain it, except when the small part of me that doesn't like being misunderstood feels a need, or if I think someone else might benefit from it. This is my humble attempt, for both reasons previously stated.

I tend to play my own compositions pretty much exclusively, and I don't do many covers, hardly any, in fact, unless it's as a soundcheck or a kick. It's not an ego thing to me, or some elitist attitude, it's just a natural compulsion that gives me no rest if I try to ignore it. I know this holds me back in the traditional sense and isolates me, which is hard to reconcile sometimes, but I really have no choice in the matter. The course was set a long time ago.

I've been writing songs and stories for as long as I can remember, way before I learned to play any instruments. Still do a few of them today. It was just a natural thing to me, not special… just natural. It was the thing that really attracted me to music and I pursued it passionately. That kinda changed when I started playing in bands.

It doesn't matter if it's an established act or a garage band, once the step is taken into the music business, certain conditions are expected to be met, certain dues paid, and nobody gets a free pass. People like to hear familiar music, agents and promotors like groups that comply with the people's desire, fellow band members prefer to eat, so writing your own material is at least not encouraged, and at worst, simply forbidden.

I understood that and went happily along with it for many years. I didn't stop writing, but didn't put much effort in it, either, usually only when I was about to burst. I did work with some folks who were open to the idea, but there is a huge difference between being open and actually getting involved. Composing is just too demanding a process to survive in an indifferent environment.

As time went by, I began to feel more and more at odds with that environment, like I was trying to fit into skinny jeans that my butt had simply outgrown. I found it harder and harder to find any joy from music and less and less a reason to remain in it. Happily for me, this feeling just happened to coincide with the arrival of a daughter into our family, and I wasn't about to let my estranged relationship with music interfere with that, so I flat quit. I didn't and don't regret a single moment of that period, nor do I regret a single one over the next several years of devoting most (all) of my time to being a parent. It was the best career move I ever made.

Another cosmic coincidence was almost too soon in coming, but come it did, and I found my duties as a parent loosening up just as my call to music returned. Older now, and far less intrigued with the thought of picking up where I left off, I did what came the most natural to me... I began writing. The songs came like never before, like the gate had swung fully open, and all those ideas and images just flowed out. It continues to be so, and the more I allow it, the more generous the flow. That brings it all up to date and full circle.

I am what I am because it's all I can be. I learned so much in my earlier years in music; I learned exactly what it takes to create a sellable product, what songs to play, what clothes to wear, what not to do. Thing is, the course that I'm compelled to take basically demands I toss all that knowledge out the window. In many ways, I'm doing the exact opposite of what I should be doing. I rarely question that contradiction because it feels so right. I instinctively know it is the only way I could ever be happy or fulfilled in music. I know that any compromise would only bring misery and discontentment.

The rare occasion that my indoctrination rears up and causes me to question my course is kinda difficult to ignore, but it never fails... *never*... that some reinforcing evidence pops up to reassure me past any idea of compromise. I wouldn't stray, but even the occasional thought of it seems to set the universe on a mission to keep me straight. Most of these reassurances come from you, the people, that, for some reason, seem to appreciate my work. Thanks for that. It's all for you anyway. So there it is, about as close as it comes to an explanation you will ever get from me.

◇

I don't know you…
but I know where you've been.

I don't know you…
but I know what you've seen.

I don't know what's happened to you;
I just know that you've changed.

It is all as it seems,
or is it a dream?

The hurt,
either way,
is the same.

◇

An Awakening

There was a time a few years ago when I truly questioned the logic in my approach to music. Indeed, I questioned my own sanity for basically ignoring the lessons learned from nearly fifty years in the music business.

To write my own material, lay it on a canvas of old, unfamiliar sounds, then render it down and refine it all to where it is solely and completely me. It is suicide for a working musician, a self-imposed exile, and a sure recipe for failure. Yet, that's exactly what I felt compelled to do, and did.

It took a lot of quiet moments in backstage dressing rooms to force this doubt from my brain long enough to step out and do a show or set. It was, at times, pure hell – as frustrating and demeaning as one can imagine just to muster up the energy to make it happen. Always having to define myself with every song. No breath or moment of occasional ease. No net.

It was so for a few months, until one particular performance opened my eyes to what had really been there all along. That realization not only answered my questions, but quenched any doubt that I was the right and true path, the only path for me.

The realization – as simple as pie and as keen as any surgeon's scalpel. In most cases, practically anybody other than me is better suited to fill the bill of a musical performance... *anybody*. However, in some cases, there is nobody on this entire planet who can fill the bill better than me... *nobody*.

The performance part of what I do is merely a search for the latter, which, to my delight, and sometimes dread, seems to come more and more frequently these days. Strange? You ought to try it from my shoes sometime.

I hope you've enjoyed your trip into my head. Please watch your step as you exit.

◇

"Song writing is very much like giving someone a gift. You know, that awkward and vulnerable moment when you place the package in someone's hands and say, 'This is for you...' Add to that, the fact that the gift is a handmade original and not a market-proven item from a gift registry list. You've asked me what it's like... there it is."

The shadows of twilight
have long since given way to the black,
velvet tide.

Time to once again pull that torn and frayed ticket stub
out of my pocket
and present it to the smiling conductor
standing,
waving
from the platform.

Peradventure
they will be serving honey cakes tonight,
with tea.

The moment is short,
but lingers
long enough
to leave you
with this
and nothing more.

Bent over backing up,
my friend,
gets your ass into places
that your heart
ain't
in.

Stand up,
move ahead,
and lead
with a smile.

Goodnight.

AFTERWORD
by Lindsay Gibson Goins

Until recently, I never completely understood exactly what my dad gave up for me. To read that I was the best career move he ever made was both humbling and heavy. No, not heavy at all... just awkward.

My dad was an extraordinary human with the ability to make you feel as though you were the only person in the world when speaking with him. He was talented, to say the least; even more than that, he was a beautiful soul – gentle, tolerant, empathetic, and down-right unique. I'll never quite grasp the reason he was taken from us so soon. However, something I know for sure is that by transcribing his words and carefully listening to his music, I have discovered so many things about him that I was previously unaware of. I've enjoyed learning about him through fresh eyes and a determined spirit.

While working on this project, there were days when I'd wake up and think, *Alright, Dad, what are you going to show me today?* It never failed that I would peel back a new layer or come up with an idea so "Scott-ish" that I simply couldn't deny his presence watching over me, sitting with me, sipping a cup of coffee; strumming a jubilant tune to keep the sorrow from creeping in. I'd like to think this project is something my dad and I worked on together.

My desire is that by reading this book you've been able to gain a piece of my dad that perhaps you didn't have in your collection before, and that the experience of his work has impacted you in some way. Whether it be a gentle nudge to explore our history, a nostalgic flashback to your childhood, a yearning for a simpler life, a calling to examine the beliefs you hold true, a caress of your spirit, or a whisper of hope. Whatever this book means to you, may it be something you treasure in memory of Scott Gibson.

To conclude, I'll leave you with a poem I wrote, inspired by my dad. I am certainly not the wordsmith he was, but I'd like to believe that this poem is a result of a wink that Dad sent down to me shortly after his passing.

Tempo Change

I had a dream last night
'Bout trouble a-comin'
What's wrong and what's right
But one thing I know
We stumble and grow
Time passes, first fast, and then slow.

You always told me to be still
Look around, wait and see
Just do what you feel
But one thing I know
We reap what we sow
Time passes, first fast, and then slow.

There's not a day that goes by
When I don't think of you
Or just question why
But one thing I know
We've got lots to show
Time passes, first fast, and then slow.

Don't fret about what has not come
Keep a song in your heart
And refuse to go numb
'Cause one thing I know
There's more hope than woe
Time passes, first fast, and then slow.

My time with you was much too short, yet the time without you seems to be moving slower with each passing each day. Good thing we'll see each other again soon... somewhere beyond Lexitown, just past the Old Dirt Road, where we'll have a standing reservation at the Table of the Lord. There, all we'll have is sweet Time, Time, Time.

LG
May 13, 2018

ACKNOWLEDGEMENTS

Thank you, Jennifer Leonard, for your work on the cover images. I feel that you truly captured a symbolic example of something that is not heavy, yet painfully awkward.

Thank you, Christopher Allred, for providing the main image on the back cover. Your appreciation for my dad's work and your ability to capture his quirkiness will be remembered always.

A special thanks goes to our Kickstarter contributors and initial supporters. Without you, we would not have been able to do any of this. I truly appreciate you all.

Thank you to Donnie Roberts for being a voice of reason and one of my dad's biggest fans.

To my mom, Kay Gibson: Thank you for putting up with me. Thanks for your encouragement and bold advice, and for bringing me back down to Earth.

To my husband, James Goins: Thank you for allowing me the time to work on this project and for being understanding of my obsession with perfection. I love you.

Thank you to our son, Taylor Goins, for being my source of inspiration. It is because of you that I wanted to do all of this. I pray that one day you will understand just how amazing your grandfather was. I hope you'll see that, in hindsight, it was all for you. May you receive this gift with open arms and develop a love for music and writing, following in the footsteps of your Pappy.

Thank you to the listeners – those of you who have allowed my dad's music to invade your ears and challenge your senses. Thanks for being one of the few who truly "got" him. Believe me, I see you.